MW01026548

Also by S. Gross

Catss by Gross
Your Mother Is a Remarkable Woman
No More Mr. Nice Guy
Love Me, Love My Teddy Bear
More Gross
An Elephant Is Soft and Mushy
I Am Blind and My Dog Is Dead
How Gross

Edited by S. Gross

Teachers Teachers Teachers
Lawyers Lawyers Lawyers
Play Ball
Moms Moms Moms
Ho Ho Ho
Movies Movies Movies
Golf Golf Golf
Books Books Books
All You Can Eat
Cats Cats Cats
Dogs Dogs Dogs
Why Are Your Papers in Order?

WE HAVE WAYS OF MAKING YOU LAUGH

120 Funny Swastika Cartoons

BY S. Gross

SIMON & SCHUSTER
New York London Toronto Sydney

"This is a wonderful opportunity for you to start thinking outside of the box."

"The original is on a teepee outside of Minot, North Dakota."

"It's an obedient wine."

"We have white mice."

"He loves to tease."

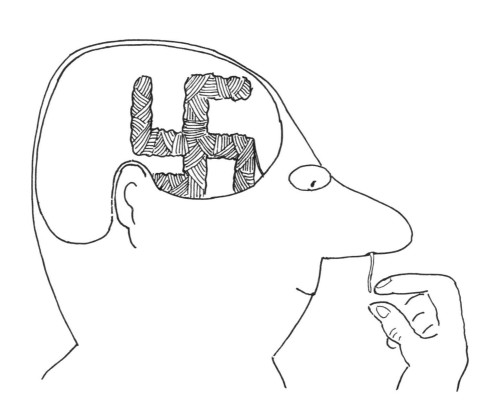

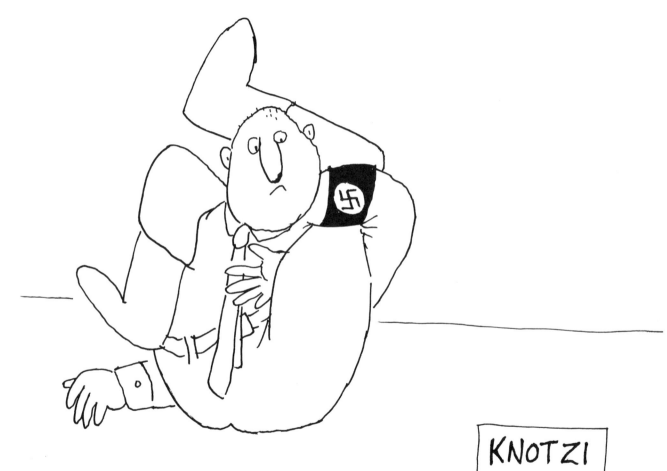

KNOTZI

*"I've had a crush on you ever since the fourth grade.
I'd be happy to carry your books to the burning."*

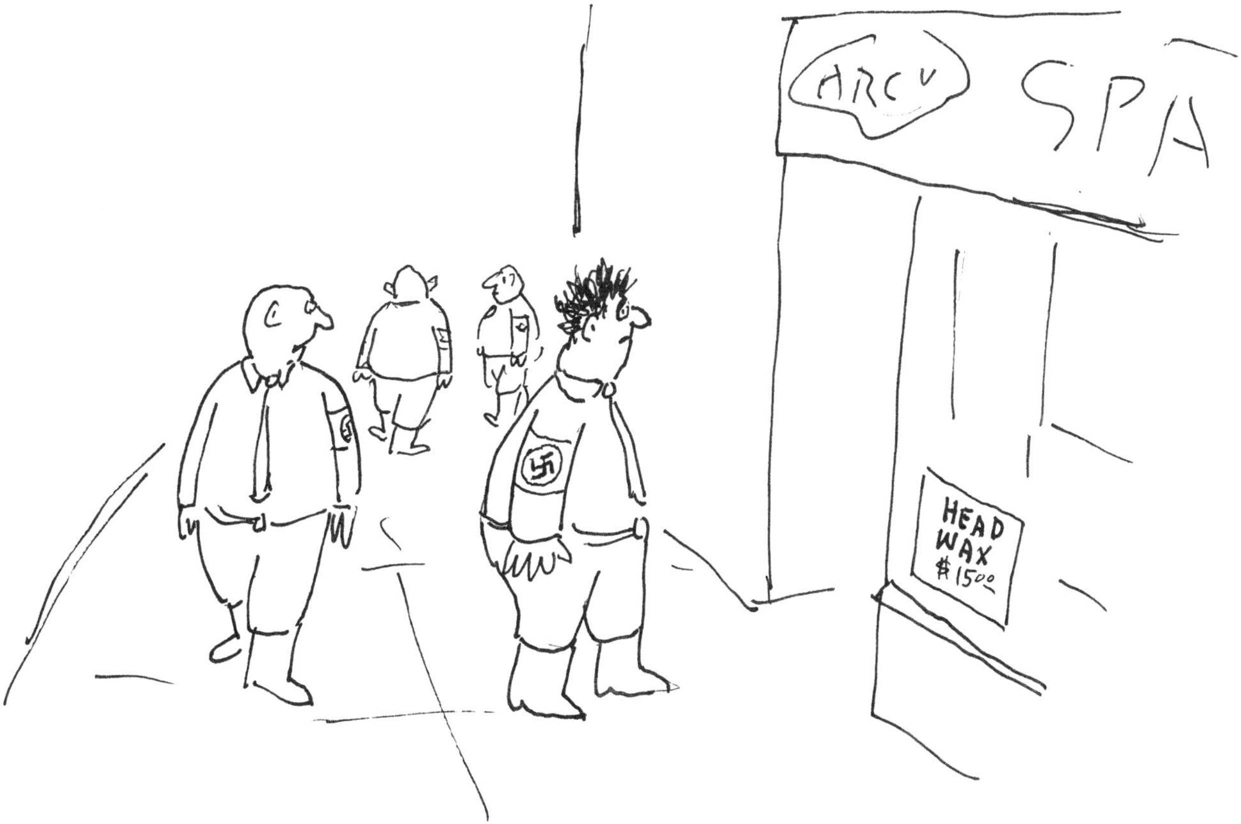
ARCU SPA
HEAD WAX $15.00

"*We got rid of one but I had to join the party.*"

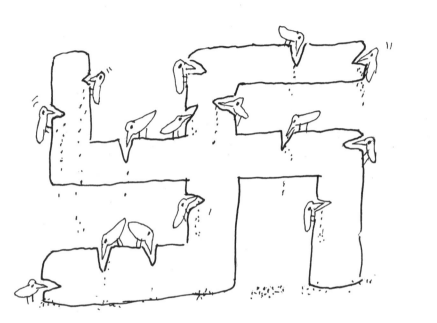

"We're going to be moving on. Too many people have been pissing on his grave."

"*He talks but only if you torture him.*"

"Eat the children!"

"Try scent marking. It's nicer."

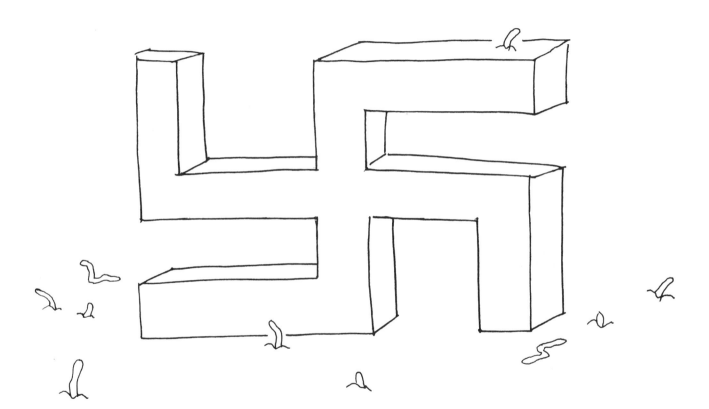

"I've been made an honorary reptile."

"Stop and smell the books."

"Are you my mommy?"

"I couldn't get him to talk."

"*We have ways of making you get new furniture.*"

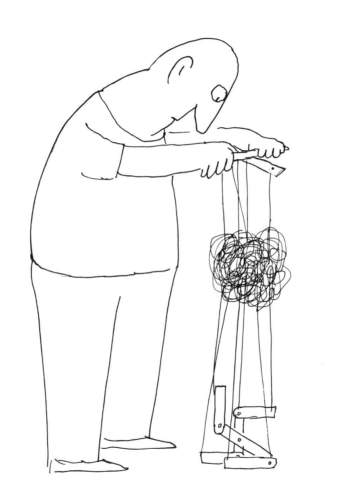

"You goose-step like a girl!"

"I have my own armband."

SCHNOZZI

"Uh, oh. You ate something that made you stupid."

LACTOSE INTOLERANT

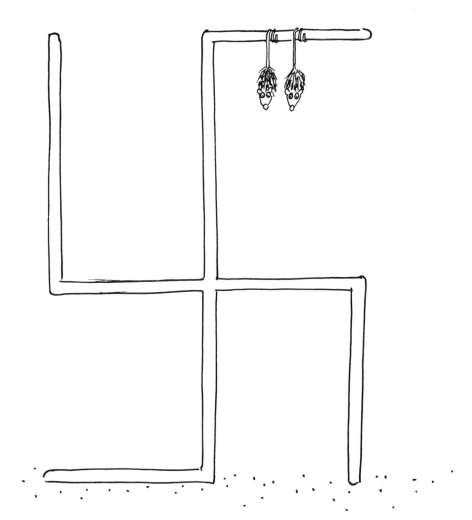

"What are you in for?"

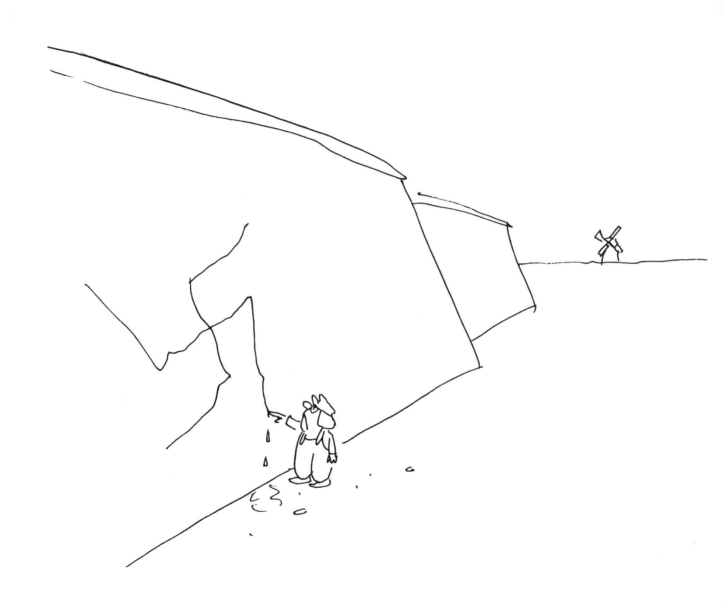

WUMP!

PAPARANAZI

"We're lovebirds. We hate you."

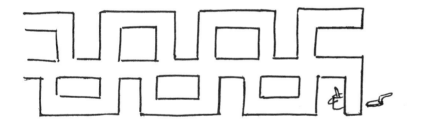

"So you're the other white meat."

"*The sleeve keeps riding up.*"

"No! This is how you do the cakewalk."

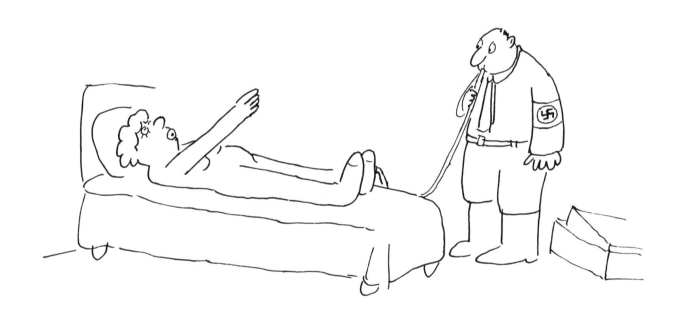

"Mother Goose is a different person. I'm Mother Goose-step."

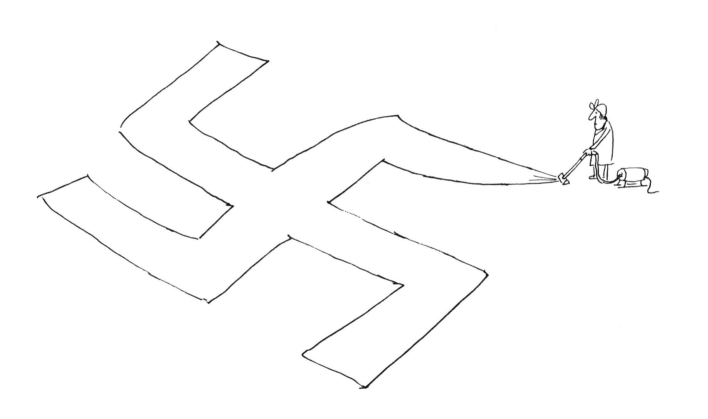

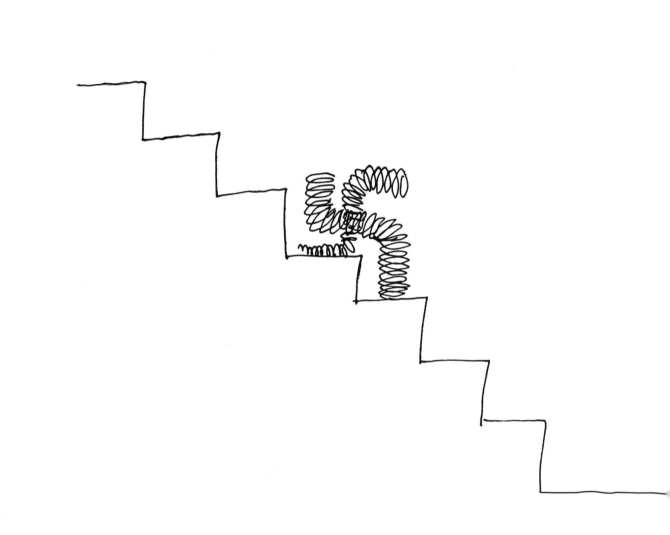

CRYPTO-NAZI

"Try it again. You almost goose-stepped."

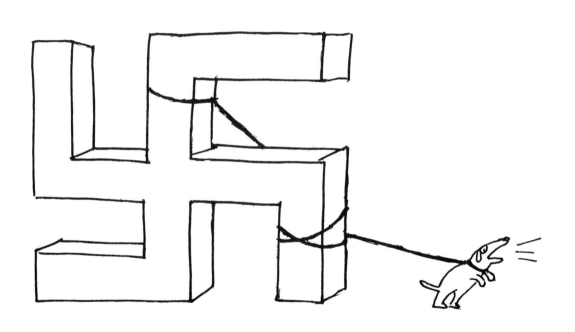

"*Act out! That's easy enough for you to say.*"

"Are you ready to start denazification?"

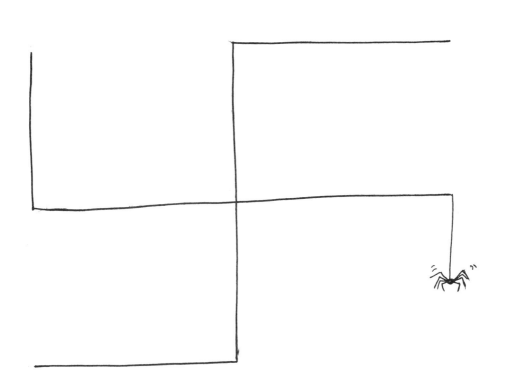

"I'll call you back. I'm trying to make the ten o'clock news."

"Why don't you go back and try again."

"I joined because you get to keep warm during the book burnings."

"It's ten o' clock. Do you know where you hid
that armband that you wore during the war?"

AFTERWORD

These drawings emerged from my involuntary reaction to a swastika shown on the news. Awareness came next and then the need to exorcise the reaction, which in my case happened to be anger. What other people's are, I can only offer conjecture.

The first drawings formed in my head during the spring of 1997 and continue to arrive sporadically. My initial intent was to allay my anger by portraying things happening to and around the swastika so as to reduce it to something humorous. If something is humorous, you can't get angry at it; nor can it inspire fear.

Simon & Schuster
1230 Avenue of the Americas
New York, NY 10020

Copyright © 2008 by Sam Gross

All rights reserved, including the right to reproduce this book or portions thereof in any form whatsoever. For infomation address Simon & Schuster Subsidiary Rights Department, 1230 Avenue of the Americas, New York, NY 10020.

First Simon & Schuster hardcover edition March 2008

SIMON & SCHUSTER and colophon are registered trademarks of Simon & Schuster, Inc.

For information about special discounts for bulk purchases, please contact Simon & Schuster Special Sales at 1-800-456-6798 or business@simonandschuster.com.

Designed by Kate Susanna Moll

Manufactured in the United States of America

1 3 5 7 9 10 8 6 4 2

Library of Congress Cataloging-in-Publication Data

Gross, S. (Sam)
We have ways of making you laugh : 120 funny swastika cartoons / by S. Gross.
p.   cm.
1. Swastikas in art.   2. American wit and humor, Pictorial.
I. Title.

NC1429.G76A4   2008
741.5'973–dc22   2007047508

ISBN-13: 978-1-4165-5640-4
ISBN-10:   1-4165-5640-0